Great Minds Start Little

baby einstein.

Great Minds Start Little

A Guide for Parents

Concept by
Julie Aigner-Clark

Text by
Marcy Kelman

Illustrations by
Nadeem Zaidi

DISNEP
EDITIONS
NEW YORK

For information address Disney Editions, 114 Fifth Avenue, New York, New York 10011-5690.

Disney Editions Editorial Director: Wendy Lefkon
Disney Editions Editor: Jody Revenson

Printed in Singapore

First Edition
10 9 8 7 6 5 4 3 2 1

Library of Congress Cataloging-in-Publication Data
Clark, Julie Aigner-
Great minds start little: a guide for parents / concept by Julie Aigner-Clark; illustrations by Nadeem Zaidi.—1st ed.
      p.   cm.
Includes bibliographic references.
ISBN 0-7868-5397-2
1. Infants. 2. Toddlers. 3. Child development. 4. Child rearing. 5. Play. 6. Educational games. I. Title.
HQ774.C53 2003
649'.1–dc21
2003043855

Visit www.disneyeditions.com

You brought your children
into this amazing world . . .
Mind if we **show them around?**

The Baby-Friendly Home

Transform your home into a baby-friendly environment that is not only safe and secure but also nurturing and accessible to little ones.

Room-by-Room the Baby Einstein Way
Create safe and inviting play areas in your child's room, the kitchen, the bathroom, and the living room with handy tips and hints for outfitting each room in the house

Creating a Child-Friendly Atmosphere
Mood-enhancing and environment-friendly ideas evoking a warm, nurturing atmosphere that encourages emotional growth and stimulation

Taking the Bore out of Chores
Novel ideas for turning household chores into teachable moments

Ten Essential Toys for Baby's Play Area
Our top-ten list of skill-building toys for your child's play area, plus detailed descriptions of how each toy nurtures your baby's intellectual, social, and emotional growth

chapter 2

Tools for Discovery page 63

Discover unique projects and one-on-one activities to encourage language development and celebrate the arts and sciences. Expert teaching practices and tried-and-true parenting tips combine to turn everyday activities into enriching learning experiences.

chapter 3

Tools for Learning page 99

The perfect library of books and music provides a comprehensive catalog of baby-friendly educational resources, including poetry anthologies, art books, and classical music. Outfit your home with a selection from this section and you'll expose your children to the greatest forms of human expression—language, poetry, music, and art.

index page 119

The Baby Einstein Philosophy

At Baby Einstein, we know that babies are curious. They're fascinated by the sights and sounds around them. And every moment of every day in a baby's early years is an opportunity for discovery. What makes babies and toddlers such delightful learners is that they are incredibly curious about and delighted by the world around them. How a plant grows from a seed, which colors are in a rainbow, and how a snowflake melts into a drop of water in your palm are all fascinating miracles to a young child.

We believe that babies and toddlers can appreciate art and the humanities. *Great Minds Start Little* provides new ways to interact with your child with innovative ideas and stimulates natural curiosity, using real world objects and exposing youngsters to music, art, language, science, poetry, and nature in playful and enriching ways.

The ideas in *Great Minds Start Little* aren't meant to make your baby or toddler "smarter." They're designed to contribute to the development of happy, healthy children and to give them what they'll never outgrow— curiosity and a capacity for wonder. Using the simple suggestions in this book, you will spark your child's creativity and imagination while fostering a love for words, music, and art that will last a lifetime.

Praise for The Baby Einstein Company

"I joined a parenting board on-line when I was pregnant, and many of the women could not stop talking about Baby Bach, Baby Mozart and Baby Einstein. Once my son was born, I had to see for myself. I purchased Baby Bach and Baby Mozart and played them for him. All of the wonderful comments those ladies on the board said could not have been more true. James was mesmerized by the music and images. He is now almost 18 months and still watches them almost daily. A couple of weeks ago, I purchased Baby Shakespeare—he said "apple" the next day! He loved it. He dances and talks back to them, but in a quiet way. I purchased Baby Van Gogh today, and he just wants me to keep rewinding! I always tell any pregnant women I know about the videos. They were definitely the most important purchases I've made for my son. Thank you!"

"All I can say is thank you, thank you, thank you! My son, Steven, is nine months old and has been enjoying your videos from three weeks of age! I can't tell you how many hours we have spent as a family watching your videos, but I can tell you that it is a very special and important part of our day. I have told every mother-to-be that these videos are a 'MUST-HAVE.' Please, continue to make these wonderful educational tools—we can't get enough!"

"On a recent trip to the USA to visit my sister who had twin boys I discovered your videos of Baby Bach and Baby Mozart. The boys were both born with severe heart defects and needed to be kept stress-free while they waited for surgery. My sister achieved this stress-free atmosphere in her house with the help of your videos. They helped the boys relax when they were fretful. They began at a very young age to recognize the pieces of music they particularly enjoyed. I play violin and when I played some of the pieces that are also on the videos you could see by their reaction that they had heard the tune before and enjoyed it. They are now over surgery and doing very well."

"I received the Baby Einstein tape as a gift from my cousin. She told me how much her son loved watching this video. I could not believe that an infant would sit and watch a video. When I had my children there was no such thing. I exposed Micayla, my granddaughter, to Baby Einstein at one week old. She and I watch it at least three times a week. Baby Einstein is her favorite. I just have to say, 'Micayla, do you want to watch your "Baby Einstein" movie?' And, she replies with a nod and claps her hands. She now is one year old and knows the video by heart (and so do I). Thank you."

Developmental Stages

One to nine months: From very early on, babies react to the sights and sounds around them, first turning in the direction of a speaker to smile at his or her face, and then mimicking vowel sounds and vocal inflections until eventually initiating their own "conversations" with coos, babbles, and squeals of delight. By nine months, babies will be able to utter consonants, recognize their name, respond to simple words like "no," and possibly say their first word. Having already mastered sitting, rolling over, and crawling, Baby is now anxious to explore her environment at eye level. She can pull herself up to a standing position and, with the aid of furniture or a helping hand, take those first few baby steps and even stand unassisted for a few seconds. She is able to uncover hidden objects, stack toys, wave "bye-bye," and do a bit of finger feeding. Best of all, she loves to bounce and rock to music.

One to Nine Months

Nine to eighteen months: By eighteen months, toddlers are proudly showing off their independence. Baby is able to walk alone forward and backward, climb on furniture, do a bit of staggered running, push and pull large objects, sip from a cup, throw toys, and fill a spoon to feed himself. He finds endless amusement in imitating actions, singing and shouting, scribbling with crayons, playing "make-believe," and giving out kisses and hugs to his favorite people. And, although he can say about 20 words, he understands the meaning of about 50!

Toddlers this age also have an increasing fascination with spatial relations, whether it's exploring how their bodies can fit under chairs and behind beds or the amazing realization that they can fill up and pour out the contents of their cup again and again.

Nine to Eighteen Months

Eighteen to thirty-six months: By the time she turns three, a child will learn to follow simple directions, be able to recognize and name her emotions, sort items by color or size, know how to use personal pronouns, and even utter three- to four-word sentences! As for motor skills, she'll be very busy kicking balls, using a paintbrush, jumping up and down in place, cutting with scissors, putting together simple puzzles, taking her own clothes off, unscrewing lids from jars, and going up and down the stairs unassisted. It's at this stage that children begin to understand the passage of time, and learn the concepts of sharing, taking turns, and other social skills.

Eighteen to
Thirty-Six Months

Introduction

Welcome to the first Baby Einstein product created for parents. As we studied our array of great books, videos, CDs, DVDs, and other enriching items, we noticed there was one little gap—a book written for the parents of newborns, infants, and toddlers. So here is *Great Minds Start Little*.

In the pages that follow, you'll find dozens of wonderful ideas, projects, and activities that will help you foster confidence, encourage self-expression, and celebrate learning with your child.

Our first chapter offers a room-by-room guide filled with simple ideas and handy hints to transform each room into an inviting, baby-friendly space. Once you've modified the rooms in your home, we offer some mood-enhancing ideas to help create a warm and nurturing atmosphere, including advice on baby massage and essential oils. And we'll even help you take the bore out of chores with some clever ideas to turn household necessities into fun times for your baby.

In "Tools for Discovery," we offer dozens of fun and easy activities and ideas that will encourage language development and celebrate the arts and sciences. From great ideas incorporating books and music to hand games and nature activities, this section combines expert teaching practices and tried-and-true parents' tips to turn everyday activities into wonderful learning experiences.

And in "Tools for Learning," discover a carefully selected listing of poetry anthologies, classical music, and books featuring great masterpieces. These resources invite your child to discover the greatest forms of human expression and set them on a magical journey that is certain to promote a lifetime love of learning.

How to Use This Book

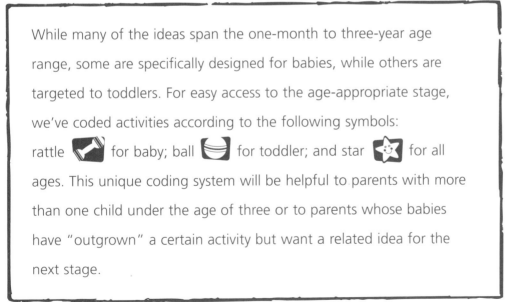

While many of the ideas span the one-month to three-year age range, some are specifically designed for babies, while others are targeted to toddlers. For easy access to the age-appropriate stage, we've coded activities according to the following symbols: rattle for baby; ball for toddler; and star for all ages. This unique coding system will be helpful to parents with more than one child under the age of three or to parents whose babies have "outgrown" a certain activity but want a related idea for the next stage.

chapter 1

The Baby-Friendly Home

Babies truly make a house a home, and once they arrive, you'll never look at your place the same way again. The heirloom crystal, porcelain knickknacks, and state-of-the-art electronic appliances that you once lovingly displayed now make you shudder with fear. Yes, the time has come to redecorate for your *new* pride and joy. And the best way to start is to venture into every room of your house just as Baby would—on your hands and knees! However, while looking for potential hazards from Baby's perspective, keep in mind that it's just as important to look for hidden learning opportunities at every turn.

Although there are some objects you definitely won't want to install at Baby's eye level, there are other items that you will—particularly those that can serve as teaching tools. This chapter contains clever ideas for transforming your home into an environment that's fun, nurturing, and inviting to little ones. Throughout your home, strategically place clever devices that will foster independence and inspire curiosity. These should be at eye level for those . . . short in stature! Because children spend most of their waking hours in rooms other than the nursery, it's important to consider the possibilities each and every room in your house has to offer. (To get you started, here's a room-by-room overview for creating safe and accessible play areas throughout your house.)

Room-by-Room the Baby Einstein Way

Your Child's Room

When decorating the nursery for your baby, keep in mind that newborns can visually perceive objects placed 8 to12 inches away from their face. Since their field of vision is limited, contrasting colors (such as combinations of red, black, and white) are easiest to discern. Create easy-to-make, engaging flash cards displaying favorite baby images, such as smiling faces, checkerboards, spirals, bull's-eyes, zigzags, diagonals, and other captivating patterns. Ensuring that flash cards are out of Baby's reach and securely affixed, add a few cards to a mobile, attach them to her crib where she can easily gaze at them, or hang them on the wall just above the diaper-

changing table. Periodically, rotate the placement of flash cards to give her a change of scenery.

Give your newborn something stimulating and adorable to look at while in the crib—himself! Fasten a child-safe, unbreakable mirror right in his crib to provide hours of delight. Faces are the most engaging images to Baby, and he'll soon realize that when he moves his head or smiles, so, too, does the face in the mirror.

Attach a pinwheel to the foot of Baby's changing table. Spin the pinwheel to keep her occupied as you change her diaper, get her undressed, or check her temperature. She'll love watching the pretty colors in motion, and it will help to distract her as you attend to the task at hand.

Hang a bulletin board on the wall above Baby's changing table and attach large magazine cutouts of baby faces—plus mommy, daddy, and grandma—using putty-tack adhesive instead of pins or thumbtacks to affix the cutouts. Point to the faces as you change him, and reinforce words such as "baby," "eyes," "nose," "smile," and "mouth." When he's older, you can use the bulletin board to showcase his drawings and paintings.

For reassuring "night-lights" in your toddler's room, consider affixing glow-in-the-dark moon and star stickers to the ceiling above his bed. Before tucking him in for the night, sing "Twinkle, Twinkle, Little Star" together, ask him to make a wish on a star, or make up a fairy tale about a brave space explorer who just happens to share your child's name. Talking about the night sky makes a wonderful bedtime ritual, and the comforting glow of the stickers will help to combat a fear of the dark.

Paint your child's closet door or a section of her bedroom wall with chalkboard paint (available at most hardware stores) for a permanent canvas on which to showcase his many doodling masterpieces. To section off the chalkboard area on the wall, first find a large wooden frame at a thrift store, paint the chalkboard area to suit the frame size, and then hot-glue the frame to the wall. Alternatively, scout out tag sales for inexpensive wooden toy cabinets or short wooden tables and cover them with chalkboard paint. Stock your child's art supplies with colored chalk and easy-to-trace plastic cookie cutters.

Create a cozy reading nook in a corner of your toddler's bedroom. Place throw pillows and beanbag chairs to create a comfy sitting area. Turn a plastic milk crate on its side to function as both a holder for favorite books and a table on which to place snacks and sippy cups. Consider using this area to read favorite bedtime or nap-time stories to your child.

Mount a large cookie sheet on your toddler's bedroom wall, positioning it at eye level, so that she can spell out fun words with magnetic alphabet letters. Buy self-adhesive magnet sheets to display magazine cutouts of babies, animals, flowers, and other images your toddler might find appealing on her magnetic play area. You might want to print out a few common vocabulary words on your computer, turn them into magnets, then sit down with your toddler to create a rebus story that combines both the images and words on her cookie sheet.

If you don't have enough floor space for an easel in your child's room, consider mounting a large, easel-sized clipboard on a wall in his room. The clipboard can hold big sheets of paper on which he can draw and finger-paint, and it won't take up any room when not in use. In fact, it can become an ever-changing display area for works of art.

Instead of storing a bulky puppet theater in your child's bedroom, place an expandable, spring-loaded curtain rod in his doorway for an instant puppet-show stage. Hang an old tablecloth or curtain set from the rod, and let him decorate it to his liking. When the puppet show is over, simply store the "stage" in a linen closet.

Kitchen

 Babies quickly become antsy when sitting in a high chair. If you find that your child is grabbing the spoon out of your hand every time you try to feed him, consider giving him his own spoon. He'll love the independence of holding his own utensil! More than likely, he will bang the spoon on the food tray, try to scoop out food from the jar you're holding, make attempts at getting the spoon into his mouth, and (best of all) even try to feed *you*. Hold off on washing his face and wiping down his high chair in between bites. This may be a messy venture, but it's important to give him the time and space needed to experiment with self-feeding. In fact, you may find that he'll actually sit and eat for a longer period of time when given his own utensils.

Another way to hold Baby's interest at mealtime is to hang an unbreakable mirror on a wall by his high chair where he can watch himself eat. He'll love opening his mouth to see what's inside, offering his reflection a bite to eat, and watching himself chew food and drink from a sippy cup. Above all, looking in a mirror will help him master the fine art of holding a spoon and successfully transporting food into his mouth.

Set aside one cabinet or drawer in your kitchen just for Baby. This will keep her occupied as you attend to daily chores and will also help curb her interest in off-limits areas of the kitchen. Stock her special storage space with a changing array of plastic cups and containers for nesting and stacking, large wooden spoons for banging and pretend mixing, and plastic funnels and measuring cups for filling and pouring.

Replace tiny kitchen magnets that could pose a choking hazard with extra-large plastic magnetic alphabet letters. Consider creating a much anticipated ritual that involves checking out the refrigerator each morning for the word of the day or a special message that you've spelled for Baby. Buy self-adhesive magnet sheets to make your own child-safe magnets, starring pictures of favorite pets, baby

faces from magazines, or securely mounted plastic cars that your toddler can "vroom" across the refrigerator.

⭐ Shop tag sales and/or thrift stores to find a plastic, child-size table-and-chairs set for your kitchen. Buy several paper tablecloths at a dollar store or discount party center. Take out a new tablecloth each week and let Baby decorate it with crayons and stickers to entertain imaginary tea-party guests. Help her come up with different decorating themes for the week, such as bugs, flowers, animals, fish, or silly faces. This project makes a wonderful Monday morning tradition, and she can add to her tablecloth masterpiece every day.

⭐ Create a "sandbox" in the kitchen. Fill a shallow, rectangular plastic bin with dry macaroni or puffed-rice cereal. Keep plastic measuring cups, colanders, bowls, and sand pails and shovels on hand for digging up and scooping out the "sand." You may want to consider burying a hidden treasure in the sandbox for your baby to find each morning, such as a favorite stuffed animal, action figure, truck, or packaged fruit snack.

⭐ Let Baby finger-paint on her high chair's food tray with a favorite flavor of pudding, yogurt, or applesauce. This is a tasty way for her to strengthen hand-eye coordination, as you show her how to trace shapes, smiley faces, numbers, and alphabet letters with her fingers.

⭐ If you have sturdy kitchen chairs, consider hanging toys from plastic chain links attached to your chairs' back rails. This is a great way to situate toys at eye level and encourage crawlers to stand up with the aid of a chair and practice the fine art of balancing.

⭐ Create an obstacle course in the kitchen for cruisers. Position four or more kitchen chairs about a foot away from one another. Place a toy atop each chair seat and watch your cruiser cautiously move from one chair to the next to investigate each exciting plaything. Once he's mastered this course, position chairs farther away from one another to give your cruiser the opportunity to take a few baby steps between them.

⭐ Rinse out yogurt containers to use as clever playthings in the kitchen. Stack several in a pyramid formation on the kitchen floor, so you can play a bowling game with Baby, using a rubber ball. You can also place dry rice in securely lidded yogurt containers for fun-to-shake rattles, or use the containers as handy, on-the-go holders for crayons or afternoon snacks.

🥣 For hours of make-believe fun, let toddlers set up shop in your kitchen. Recycle empty cereal boxes, oatmeal containers, soda bottles, coffee canisters, and egg cartons for their pretend grocery store. They can use a cardboard

General Store

box as a front counter, food-shaped magnets or plastic toy foods from tag sales, paper bags for bagging all the items, a wagon as a grocery cart, and paper money made from green construction paper.

Bathroom

Take time to show Baby how things work in the bathroom. Run some warm water from the faucet, let her move her hands back and forth under the stream, and then dry off her hands with a soft towel. Show her how the toilet flushes, how you brush your teeth, how she can try out her own baby toothbrush, and how to brush your hair and her hair in the mirror.

Look for child-safe step stools at tag sales and thrift stores. Take time to paint the stool in her favorite color, personalize it with her name, and add decorative touches with glitter glue and silver and gold paint pens. A stepping stool will make your child self-sufficient, providing her with access to the sink and mirror when she needs to brush her teeth, comb her hair, or wash her hands and face. Make sure you keep her stepping stool in a closet or cabinet when not in use, and ask her to let you know when she needs it. This safety precaution will ensure that you are always present when she climbs up on it.

⭐ You don't need to purchase a slew of commercial bath toys to make a splash in the tub—watered-down favorites can be found right in your kitchen. In fact, the items from Baby's personal storage space in the kitchen can serve double duty in the bathtub. Plastic cups, funnels, pitchers, measuring spoons, and small food containers are great choices for filling up and pouring out water.

⭐ Let kids go on a fishing trip right in the tub. Use permanent markers to turn old plastic measuring spoons into colorful fish and other aquatic creatures. Children will enjoy scooping up their catches of the day with a kitchen strainer to serve as their fishing net.

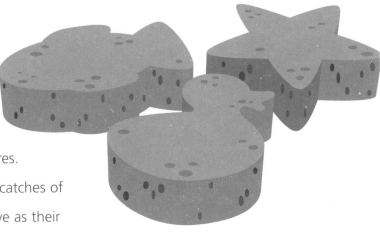

⭐ Cut out ducks, turtles, frogs, dolphins, and starfish from new sponges, using cookie cutters. Let Baby feel the rough, porous texture of a dry sponge before plunging it into the water so the child can watch it magically expand in size. Talk about how the sponge takes on a squishy texture when wet. Encourage him to wring out water from the sponge, then fill it up with water and watch it grow.

⭐ Use scissors to turn a terry-cloth towel into a fun washcloth shaped like an octopus or jellyfish. Be sure to cut long strips from the towel to create long, dangling legs for the creature. Make it wiggle, jiggle, and chase after Baby underwater, then let the creature's dangling legs crawl up Baby's legs, arms, and head for a silly tickle game.

⭐ Plastic soap dishes and margarine containers make terrific bath-time boats, while square plastic container lids make ideal rafts for carrying small plastic figures. For ring-shaped flotation devices, let action figures float inside a few of Baby's plastic stacking rings.

A bath is the perfect opportunity to teach Baby about her body parts. Create silly rhymes to teach her their names:

*"After dinner it's such a messy place,
so now it's time to wash your face.*

*I've got a rhyme, and here it goes:
I love to scrub your cute little nose!*

*Is it dirty? Let's go and check,
and wash and clean sweet (NAME)'s neck.*

*Yes, my baby has such charm,
with soapsuds up and down her arm.*

*It's very cute and shakes like jelly.
Yes-siree, that's my (NAME)'s belly.*

*I hope you don't think me a pest,
but now it's time to wash your chest.*

*Wash those legs, scrub those knees—
I'll wash those feet now, if you please.*

*Now we shampoo (NAME)'s hair,
then rinse her off with the greatest care."*

⭐ For a bath-time hand puppet, cut off the fingers of a rubber glove and draw a silly face on the palm of the glove. Wear the glove on your hand and animate it by wiggling your fingers, tickling Baby, giving the face a beard and hair with soap bubbles, making the puppet swim, and using a funny voice as your gloved character washes Baby.

⭐ Hang a visually stimulating toy from your shower spout, using plastic chain links. To prevent soap from getting in her eyes, direct your baby's attention to the toy hanging above her when it's time to rinse her hair.

⭐ For some squeaky-clean fun, here's a great song to sing while washing Baby with those foamy bath-time bubbles:

> **"Bubbles, bubbles in the tub,**
> **Baby needs a rub-a-dub scrub.**
> **Bubbles, bubbles in the air,**
> **On your back, and in your hair.**
> **Bubbles, bubbles so much fun,**
> **Rinse them off, and bath time's done!"**

⭐ Hanging an unbreakable mirror from your tub spout, so that it's at eye level when Baby's taking a bath, will make even the shyest bathers come out of their shells. They'll love playing peekaboo in the mirror with a facecloth, giggling at bubble beards on their face, and splashing at their reflection. For big laughs, give a spiky shampoo hairdo or make soapy hair stand up on end in the center of the head.

⭐ Pour clear, liquid baby soap into several paper cups and add a few drops of food coloring to each. Dip your fingers into the soap mixtures to paint Baby's skin with colorful swirls, letters, shapes, smiley faces, and zigzags. As you dab on each color, tell Baby what you're doing: "Let's paint Baby's arm red" or "Now we're painting a blue face on Baby's belly." When you're done with your painting session, simply rinse off the soap.

⭐ For true watercolors in the bath, fill three spray bottles with water and add a few drops of red food coloring to one, yellow to another, and blue to the third. Have fun spraying these splashy primary colors onto your bathroom's tile or plastic walls. Talk about the colors as you spray them and mix a few splashes together to show how primary colors combine to create hues of green, purple, and orange.

Living Room

Instead of spending money on activity gyms for your living room, position two sturdy wooden chairs, back to back, about four feet away from each other. Insert a broom through the rails of the chairs, so that the broom handle rests on the seat of one chair and the "brush side" sits on the other. Attach several plastic chain links to the middle of the broom, adding a toy to the bottom link of each chain. Once toys are in place, use duct tape to secure broom to the seats of the chairs. Position a soft blanket under the toy chains, so that Baby can reach for and play with the hanging toys while resting comfortably on her back.

Make sure you have a CD or cassette player in the living room. Children of all ages love to sway and rock to music, so keep a varied collection of CDs on hand. In addition to moving to classical music, dance with your baby to reggae, jazz, and favorite rock-and-roll tunes. Baby

Einstein videos and DVDs also feature great musical selections for dancing. See how he reacts and moves to a wide array of beats and melodies. Listen to upbeat jazz rhythms to lift the spirits of a fussy or teething baby, or gently lull tired Baby into dreamland, using New Age music infused with sounds from nature, like caressing ocean waves or the soothing night songs of crickets.

⭐ Keep a short, toy-filled laundry basket in the living room for little ones to pull out and play with at their leisure. Most babies love sitting in the basket and will spend more time climbing in and out of it than actually playing with the toys themselves. Take this opportunity to teach Baby about "full" and "empty" and "in" and "out," as she fills up, then empties out the basket of toys.

⭐ Remove breakable items from the bottom two shelves of a bookshelf or cabinet and fill them with Baby's books, blocks, and toys to give him his own personal storage space in the living room. Babies always seem to receive more toys than they can possibly play with at one sitting, so why not present them with a new

toy collection in their toy storage area every few days or so? For example, divide 21 favorite toys and stuffed animals into three baskets (labeled "A," "B," and "C"), each filled with seven toys. For afternoon playtime on Monday and Tuesday, set out basket "A" on his shelf. Bring out basket "B" for Wednesday and Thursday, and let Baby play with basket "C" on Friday and Saturday. Mix up items from baskets on Sunday and start the "toy shuffle" all over again. He'll find new ways to combine and interact with the toys each time and will never get bored with the same old collection.

Create exploration tunnels in your living room. Remove flaps from tall cardboard boxes and lay them on their sides for crawlers to venture into. Roll a ball into the tunnel for your baby to chase after, or place stuffed animals inside for her to find. Consider using duct tape to attach two tunnels together. Cut out fun shapes along the sides of the boxes using cookie cutters and a utility knife to let in light and provide peekaboo windows, then use as a primer for learning about shapes.

Paper plates can serve as terrific learning tools for toddlers. Keep a stack of decorated plates in the living room. Use markers to add alphabet letters to one set of plates, numbers to another, and splashes of color to yet another. Create an obstacle course in the living room, asking your toddler to step on the plate marked "1," for example; then move on to "2," and so on, until he gets to plate "10." He may enjoy counting down the numbers 10 to 1, walking backward to step on the plates. To teach the letters of the alphabet, place your lettered set of plates in a circle and let your toddler jump on letters as you sing the "ABC" song. Use your set of colored plates to reinforce names of colors, body parts, and the concept of left and right: "Can you touch the green plate with your right foot?"

Throw down pillows and cushions on the living room floor, so that toddlers can play leapfrog. The object is to hop from one pillow to the next without getting "wet" (touching the living room floor). This game refines dexterity and balance. If cushions seem a bit cumbersome and difficult for

your toddler to manage, substitute colorful place mats or bath towels. For a challenge, use old washcloths or table coasters for tiptoeing on the "lily pads."

 Excite adventurous crawlers by placing a large cushion on the floor in front of your sofa or love seat. Sit on the couch with a favorite book or toy and encourage Baby to climb up on the couch and sit next to you. She'll enjoy the thrill of completing the task all on her own and will love viewing the living room from a whole new perspective. Be sure to remove cushions from the floor when you're not in the room.

 Drape a large comforter over two or more sturdy wooden chairs to

create an instant make-believe house for toddlers' dolls and stuffed animals. The chair seats can serve as upstairs bedrooms, while the floor beneath the comforter and under the chairs can be turned into kitchen, dining, and living room areas. To help them decorate their homes, supply shoe boxes for beds, facecloths for quilts, sponges for pillows, and a host of small plastic containers for make-believe tables, chairs, couches, and bathtubs.

Creating a Child-Friendly Atmosphere

Now that you have a room-by-room overview for outfitting your home with actual baby-friendly features, here are some mood-enhancing and environment-friendly ideas for evoking a warm, nurturing atmosphere in your home:

Babies thrive on routines. Knowing what to expect next is very reassuring, and you can help Baby associate daily rituals with song cues. Playing a favorite *Baby Bach* or *Baby Mozart* CD selection at bath time every night, for example, will signal to Baby that it's time to wind down and transition into getting-ready-for-bed mode. Pore through your *Baby Einstein* CD collection to select just the right sound track for Baby's playtime, mealtime, or quiet cuddle time with Mom.

Choose a dimly lit area of your house that's free of distractions to feed your newborn. Shut out the stresses of your day and bask in this special bonding time: stroke Baby's face, talk about your day together, play a soothing Baby Einstein CD, and enjoy cradling your little one.

Infant massage is said to promote restful sleep, heighten self-assurance, promote weight gain, aid in digestion, and stimulate neural connections to boost brain development and intelligence. Massage is also a fun and relaxing way to bond with Baby, develop trust, and familiarize her with her own body.

After bath time or before bedtime, give Baby a calming massage using only very gentle pressure with baby oil or lotion. Make sure you massage her in a warm, dimly lit room that's free of distractions. You may want to place her on a soft towel on her changing table or on a cozy blanket on top of your bed. Select the same piece of classical music to play at each massage session. The melody will signify that it's time to wind down for the evening and prepare for the bedtime routine.

Alternatively, sing your own soothing lullaby as you massage Baby. You may want to try out this song, which follows the tune of "Here We Go 'Round the Mulberry Bush":

> **"This is the way we rub our toes,**
> **rub our toes, rub our toes.**
> **This is the way we rub our toes**
> **before we go to bed."**

Continue singing about each of the body parts as you massage them.

When babies get fussy or cranky, a change of scenery can work wonders. Hang wind chimes from a tree in your backyard. Take Baby outside to listen to the soothing notes and touch the chimes. This simple distraction can help calm his nerves and let you both enjoy a tranquil stroll outdoors.

Set up a bird feeder just outside your window, so that your baby can enjoy the magical sights and sounds of your many backyard birds. Use Baby Einstein's *Birds* and *What Does Violet See?* books as a springboard for teaching fascinating facts about birds.

It's never too early to teach the importance of recycling, and there are plenty of fun, kid-friendly ways to practice it. When you're finished with your diaper wipes, their lidded containers make clever storage boxes for crayons, markers, chalks, paintbrushes, colored pencils, and other art supplies for toddlers. Turn old shoe boxes into imaginary buildings and trains, or use them to hold toy cars or trading card collections, or cover several with construction paper to create colorful stacking blocks. Encourage your youngsters to come up with imaginative ways for transforming old magazines, newspapers, boxes, and food containers into one-of-a-kind items. You'll be surprised by their creative suggestions!

Create a relaxing, harmonious environment in your home, using the fragrant, restorative magic of essential oils. Like adults, children can benefit greatly from aromatherapy. Scent is a powerful trigger that can uplift and energize their spirits, or comfort and reassure children when they're feeling out of sorts. Roman chamomile and lavender have been used for centuries to treat anxiety, colic, teething pain, and digestive problems in children. Their sweet aromas and calming, sedative properties are ideal for pacifying tired or fussy babies.

Essential oils are available at many health-food stores and through many aromatherapy or health and beauty catalogs. Be sure to purchase only the pure essential oils and not the synthetic aromatic blends. Never apply essential oils directly to a baby's sensitive skin: always dilute first with water or mix with a carrier oil, such as jojoba or sweet almond oil, before using. To err on the side of caution, you must check with your pediatrician before trying any of these applications:

• Roman chamomile has sedative properties, making it ideal for calming children who are anxious, fearful, or having difficulty sleeping. Add one or two drops to a diffuser or onto a pillow or blanket in your child's room just before bedtime, to promote restful sleep.

• For a relaxing and sweet-smelling bath, mix a drop or two of lavender essential oil into liquid soap before adding it to the bathwater. Regularly adding lavender (or Roman chamomile) to your child's bath can help to prevent diaper rash.

• Create a warm and sunny atmosphere in your home by infusing it with citrus scents. Simply add a few drops of mandarin, grapefruit, or lemon essential oil to a lamp ring diffuser, and enjoy the uplifting effects. Mandarin is known to calm restless children and create a joyful, energized mood; grapefruit soothes anger, boosts confidence, and curbs depression; and lemon's lively scent promotes mental clarity and reduces anxiety.

• Soak a washcloth in chamomile tea, then refrigerate. Let Baby chew on the chilled washcloth to relieve teething pain.

• A hot compress, using one or two drops of Roman chamomile or lavender essential oil, may soothe earaches. Place hot compress against ear and surrounding jaw and neck areas.

• In addition to its sedative properties, chamomile is also known for its ability to aid digestion. A teaspoon or two of chamomile tea can help to relieve intestinal cramping in colicky babies.

• To soothe frayed nerves or induce a peaceful sleep (or both!), massage Baby with this luxuriant oil: 1 drop lavender essential oil, 1 drop Roman chamomile essential oil, and 5 tablespoons sweet almond oil. Gassy and colicky babies will definitely benefit from a gentle tummy massage with this calming mixture that's sure to relieve gas pressure and pain.

• For children six months and older showing signs of a cold, add a drop or two of eucalyptus smithii (the safest, most effective eucalyptus for children) essential oil to a humidifier to help relieve stuffy noses and chest congestion. Using eucalyptus in your homemade cleaning sprays and in room diffusers will help to disinfect your home and prevent the spread of cold germs among family members.

Easing the Separation

If Baby's grandparents live far away, ask them to send videotaped messages to Baby. This is a great way for Baby to link visual images to the words "Grandma" and "Grandpa." Since their faces and voices will become familiar to her through videotapes, Grandma and Grandpa will be quickly recognized—and Baby may even have an easy time saying their names—when they come to visit.

Place two drops of lavender essential oil on a handkerchief and place it near a fan or heater to release the oil's calming scent into the air when you are feeding Baby, cuddling with her, or reading a bedtime story. She'll soon begin to link this familiar scent to feelings of warmth, security, and comfort. This will help to put her at ease in unfamiliar settings (at the baby-sitter's house or in a hotel when on a family vacation) if you pack a lavender-scented handkerchief for the time away from home.

Buffer the separation anxiety your child may experience when Mom or Dad is away on business trips. Videotape Mom or Dad reading favorite books, singing songs, and blowing kisses to their little one.

Many babies and toddlers are fine during the day when in the care of a baby-sitter or relative, but will start to get homesick or anxious as evening approaches. If they'll be spending the night at Grandma's or a sitter's home, help prepare them for the nighttime transition. Tape-record the familiar and reassuring sounds of your nightly routine: songs you sing to Baby during bath time, silly games you play when getting into pajamas or brushing teeth, bedtime stories and nursery rhymes that you or Dad read to him, and favorite lullabies to sing him to sleep.

Taking the Bore Out of Chores

Unfortunately, a parent's day can't consist of all play and no work. The good news is that you don't have to cram all of your housework time into Baby's one or two one-hour nap-time intervals. For Baby, watching or helping you work around the house *is* play. Here are some novel ideas for turning household chores into fun teachable moments:

When you need to get chores done around the house, don't fret: housework may be dull and tiresome to you, but the sounds, sights, and movement involved in your daily grind are sure to fascinate Baby. Simply prop Baby in his car seat and consider mundane tasks—unloading the dishwasher, making dinner, folding laundry, and mopping the floor— prime opportunities to point out new words and phrases. Let Baby feel the warmth of clothes fresh out of the dryer, demonstrate "open" and "close" as you put items away in cabinets and drawers, and teach him the names of basic kitchen utensils, such as "cup," "plate," and "spoon." Talking to Baby as you work can help teach grammar in context and expose him to simple sentence structures, such as "Mommy dries the dishes," "I sweep the floor," and "Please, feed the dog."

sock

shirt

pants

Help your child learn new vocabulary words as you do the laundry! Teach the names of articles of clothing as you fold socks, bibs, and underwear, and hang up shirts, pants, and dresses. Consider bringing the laundry basket in front of a mirror, putting a clean sock, bib, or facecloth on Baby's head, and asking, "What's that on Baby's head? Is that a sock? Can you give the sock to Mommy?" Point out the colors of clothes and towels, then ask Baby, "Can you find the blue towel?"

A short laundry basket makes a perfect basketball hoop for Baby. While you're hanging up clothes, Baby can work on his hand-eye coordination by helping you put socks away in the laundry basket. Roll up clean pairs of socks into individual balls. Show Baby how to toss them into the basket and praise him every time he makes a basket. You can also let your toddler try to match socks by size or by color.

Attend to your morning chores and keep your toddler occupied with this daily ritual: fill a plastic lidded box with common child-safe items that all begin with the same letter (such as a banana, ball, block, and other items beginning with the letter "B"). Keep the box in the kitchen drawer or cabinet that you've set aside just for him. He'll look forward to opening the box each morning to guess the day's "mystery letter." Expose him to other objects that start with same letter throughout the day, whether you're doing chores in the backyard, driving in the car, or out grocery shopping together.

Keep your toddler busy while you work in the kitchen by playing sensory guessing games. Have her close her eyes and guess the sound you're making in the kitchen (water running, stove-door opening, broom sweeping, oven-timer bell going off); let her explore different textures with her fingers and guess what she's feeling (wiggly gelatin, squishy sponge, smooth rubber glove, rough kitchen towel); play a mystery smells game (cinnamon, apple pie, licorice, orange); or have her guess the delectable ingredients you're using to make dinner by playing a taste-test game.

In addition to helping you scoop, stir, and pour while preparing meals, your toddler can also get a handle on measurements and counting items when playing the role of assistant chef. Although he's not quite ready to divide recipes and use fractions, by working with kitchen tools that measure volume (teaspoons, tablespoons, and cups), he'll have a strong grasp on quantity discernment and a working knowledge of "small" and "big," and "less" and "more." Cooking also affords him the opportunity to, for example, practice scooping out 3 cups of flour, and counting each one aloud as he pours them into the mixing bowl.

Toddlers don't yet realize that cleanup time is an often boring, laborious task for adults. Enlisting their help during chore time will instill the importance of teamwork, responsibility, following directions, and keeping their environment tidy and orderly. It will also let them practice those all-important sorting, ordering, and matching skills they've been developing.

By the end of the day, your living room and kitchen floors have probably been redecorated with blocks, trucks, rattles, plastic containers, and pots and pans. Before it's time to get dinner preparations underway, be sure to announce, "Okay, it's cleanup time!" Encourage your child to put toys back on the shelves in her play area; wipe down her child-sized table and chair set; sort blocks, balls, and art supplies into individual bins; and return her set of kitchen utensils and containers to her personal storage space in the kitchen. Let her play copycat as she watches you work, by supplying her with a bucket of her own cleaning supplies: dust rags, sponges, a spray bottle of water, and a child-sized broom.

To keep your toddler busy while you set the table for dinner, ask her to get ready her own child-sized table for her imaginary dinner guests. As you clean off the dining room table and tidy up the odds and ends that have accumulated on it throughout the day, she can put away the toys in her imaginary eating area and wipe down the tabletop with a sponge and water. As you put out plates and silverware, encourage her to set her table with her child-sized dishes, play utensils, and tea set. She can then put her doll and teddy bear friends in their respective seats.

Ten Essential Toys
for Baby's Play Area

Many of the best educational tools are probably already in your home. The following is a top-ten list of skill-building toys for your baby's play area, along with information on how each toy will benefit your

Baby Einstein. You'll find easy and inexpensive ideas for making or utilizing many of these playthings in the "Tools for Discovery" section:

Rattles: A handheld rattle is probably the first toy you'll introduce to your child. They are easy for clenching fists to grasp and have the added bonus of making sound. In addition to developing and strengthening Baby's hand-eye coordination, rattles are wonderful tools for teaching babies how to coordinate sound and sight and distinguish and assimilate sounds. One-month-olds will often turn their gaze in the direction of a noise—a perfect opportunity to play games that employ their auditory skills. Place Baby in his car seat, shake the rattle to his left or right side, and ask, "Where's the noise?" Watch him turn his head to follow the noise and see his eyes light up when he tracks the source of the sound.

Like handheld rattles, wrist rattles and foot rattles are also wonderful devices for helping babies comprehend cause and effect. They, too, teach Baby that for every action (shaking his hand or kicking his foot), there's a reaction (the fun "chika-chika" sound of his rattle) and a sense of accomplishment.

Balls: Balls are inexpensive toys that will amuse kids of all ages. Learning to roll, throw, drop, and bounce balls improves coordination, motor skills, and muscle development. And the simple act of rolling a ball back and forth with your baby will teach her about cooperation and taking turns. Let Baby explore balls of various sizes, colors, and texture, like fuzzy, yellow tennis balls; red rubber balls; soft and squishy fabric balls; and smooth, multicolored beach balls.

Babies unable to sit up on their own can strengthen neck control and visual tracking during tummy time by watching you slowly move a ball in front of their line of vision. Crawlers will enjoy chasing after balls you throw for them. Once they can throw the ball, be sure to return the favor! Watching you crawl after balls they've thrown will make them giggle with delight. In fact, your enthusiasm for the game may spark a crawling race to the ball.

If your baby can stand in her crib, try this game: sit on the floor in front of your baby's crib and throw a fabric ball into the crib while she's there. Encourage her to pick it up and throw it back to you. Once she's mastered this, sit her on the floor with you and demonstrate how to make dunk shots into a short laundry basket.

Puzzles: Although your baby isn't quite ready for 100-piece, interlocking jigsaw puzzles, he'll certainly enjoy playing with wooden puzzles featuring whole-object pieces that fit into individual, corresponding slots on a tray. These large wooden shapes, often fitted with easy-to-grasp pegs, are ideal for exercising Baby's pincer grip, sharpening manual dexterity, and practicing fine motor skills. Puzzles encourage concentration, logical thinking, and problem-solving skills, teaching Baby how individual parts work together to form a whole. As he rotates the puzzle pieces to fit into the appropriate slots, he'll develop an awareness of spatial relationships. Above all, he'll experiénce a sense of accomplishment and pride in performing a task on his own. Look for themed puzzle trays depicting recognizable images of everyday objects, such as vehicles, toys, food, animals, flowers, or simple geometric shapes. Puzzles are ideal for kids of all ages. Preschoolers will enjoy playing with more complex puzzles that use five or six smaller pieces to complete an image.

Bubbles: Bubbles are magical to babies! Newborns will follow them with their eyes as they float across the room, honing their ability to focus on and visually track objects, while older babies will exercise their eye-hand coordination, reaching out to pop the bubbles with their fingers. Toddlers will chase after them, trying to catch them in their hands or squash them beneath their feet.

Encourage Baby to blow bubbles; the ability to blow air is an oral motor skill that will help him learn to speak later. Bubble-blowing also teaches an important lesson in patience: blowing too hard and quickly into the wand will blow the solution out of the wand before a bubble is formed, but measured and steady breaths will create large, well-formed bubbles. By the same token, kids will learn how to take turns with the bubble wand, and how important it is to wait patiently for the bubble to actually leave the bubble wand before poking it (so that it doesn't pop in the blower's eyes).

Toy instruments: Children seem to have a natural love of music. It engages them emotionally, creatively, physically, and vocally, and stimulates creative right-brain activity. Don't wait to introduce the enriching power of music to your baby. In fact, playing an instrument (even a toy instrument) for a newborn will elicit big smiles, excited kicks, and squeals of delight as she sings along to the music. Sitting babies will practice balancing their weight as they sway to the music; crawlers will practice redistributing their weight as they rock back and forth on all fours; while walkers will swing their arms, squat up and down, and move their feet to dance with you.

Help your baby discover the thrill of making music with her own hands—it's a great lesson in self-esteem and is ideal for sparking creativity, learning how to keep time, and exploring rhythmic patterns that will set the stage for language skills. Kazoos, horns, and other "wind" instruments help refine lip closure, strengthen tongue muscles, and enhance speech development. Xylophones, pianos, drums, guitars, tambourines, and other manual instruments increase dexterity, build coordination, and engage fine and gross motor skills.

Blocks: Kids love to stack, sort, knock over, bang, and build with blocks. Through trial and error, babies learn just how high they can stack blocks, gaining an early insight into scientific principles, such as balance, stability, weight, gravity, and symmetry. These simple cubes also encourage self-esteem, creativity, and independent thinking, as they strengthen Baby's hand and finger muscles. Toddlers will spend hours carefully constructing miniature houses, pyramids, bridges, trucks, skyscrapers, and rocket ships. Colorful alphabet blocks are terrific for spelling out simple vocabulary words, teaching the alphabet song, and learning to sort according to colors or letters.

Shape sorters: Recognizing and matching up common shapes is an important problem-solving skill that can be practiced with shape sorters—toys that encourage children through trial and error to match 3-D geometric objects to corresponding holes on a box. Shape sorters refine dexterity, teach cause and effect, and can help introduce the concepts of "empty" and "full" and "in" and "out."

Dolls, puppets, and stuffed animals: No play area would be complete without a multitude of fuzzy, silly, and cuddly dolls, puppets, and stuffed animals. Aside from being cute and lovable, these toys can teach babies about body awareness, help them act out imaginative stories, initiate role-playing games, expose them to new words, and introduce social skills. Dolls and puppets are wonderful tools for describing emotions, identifying parts of the body, and teaching verbs (such as "sit," "jump," "dance," "spin," and "brush hair"). Use stuffed animals to teach animal sounds and talk about each animal's habitat and special traits.

Imaginary play can also help children develop an understanding of everyday social behavior. Children usually take on adult roles when playing pretend or imitating tasks they see their parents perform throughout the day: feeding Baby, talking on the phone, driving a car, getting ready for work, washing dishes, and giving hugs. Use dolls to demonstrate empathy ("Dolly is sad. Let's give her a hug to make her feel better."); find solutions to problems ("Teddy bear looks chilly. What should we do for him?"); and teach etiquette ("Could I, please, borrow a teacup? Thank you for sharing!").

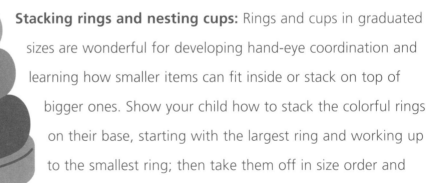

Stacking rings and nesting cups: Rings and cups in graduated sizes are wonderful for developing hand-eye coordination and learning how smaller items can fit inside or stack on top of bigger ones. Show your child how to stack the colorful rings on their base, starting with the largest ring and working up to the smallest ring; then take them off in size order and start over. Do the same with nesting cups, stacking them in graduated order until the smallest cup is in place. These toys present mathematical concepts in a fun and colorful way: children use spatial reasoning and problem-solving skills to sort and order rings and cups according to size. Nesting and stacking toys will help you introduce the concepts of "top" and "bottom," "over" and "under," and "above" and "below," "biggest" and "smallest," and "small," "medium," and "large." Be sure to purchase durable, plastic rings and cups in a variety of colors. Identify the colors as Baby stacks them. Because they're plastic, they make wonderful bath-time companions and chew toys for teething babies.

Toy vehicles: As babies become mobile, wheeled toys that can keep pace with them soon become favorite fixations. Toys that glide away from baby encourage her to follow and crawl after them. Pushing and pulling them helps to improve balance and coordination. If your child encounters an obstacle when gliding her pull toy along the floor, she must employ

problem-solving skills for overcoming and removing the obstacle from the pull toy's course. Toy cars, trucks, fire engines, buses, tractors, and wagons range in size from tiny, die-cast models to large, ride-on vehicles, so be sure to check product labels carefully to select an age-appropriate toy.

In addition to developing fine and gross motor skills, vehicles stimulate the imagination and encourage exploratory and imitative play. Above all, playing with toy vehicles promotes an interest in science. Children learn about speed, force, distance, direction, spinning mechanisms, and motion. Run simple experiments with the vehicles, pushing cars of varying sizes and weights across the floor to see which one will go the farthest, which one is the fastest, and which is the slowest.

Toy vehicles are also perfect for teaching opposites, such as "push" and "pull," "fast" and "slow," "left" and "right," "up" and "down," and "backward" and "forward." Dump trucks, wagons, and other vehicles that transport items are great for demonstrating "in" and "out" and "empty" and "full." Use vehicles to teach older children about various occupations: firefighters, police, ambulance drivers, delivery people, and construction workers.

chapter 2

Tools for Discovery

Unlike adult fun, play in Baby's world serves a unique purpose: the discovery of new skills. Each day children grow more confident in their abilities as their understanding of the world deepens. The sweet scents of a garden, the refreshing taste of a snowflake, the warmth of clothes just out of the dryer, the chatter of birds right outside the window, or the fiery orange sun setting at dusk are all magical learning experiences for a child. With fun and easy activities that encourage language development and celebrate the arts and sciences, this chapter combines expert teaching practices with tried-and-true parenting tips for turning everyday activities into enriching learning experiences.

A Star Is Born

Reinforce words you use on a daily basis with a special picture book starring Baby. Take photos of Baby performing her everyday routine: capture her feeding herself in her high chair, playing with stacking rings, taking a bath, napping in her crib, and spending time with playmates or pets. Mount the photos in a sturdy scrapbook and add captions to create a story line that follows Baby throughout the day. For a book that is sure to become a favorite bedtime story, save a photo of Baby asleep in her crib for the last page of your book. Add a caption that's sure to elicit a happy ending to the evening: "Time for sweet Hannah to close her eyes and go to bed. Good night, Hannah."

Take pictures at your next play date of Baby and her friends enjoying different activities—bouncing balls, shaking rattles, blowing bubbles, stacking blocks, and playing instruments. Place the photos in a photo album that you've entitled "My Friends." Look through the album together, pointing to Baby's playmates, saying their names, and explaining what they're doing: "There's Amelia. She's playing with a blue ball." Add photos to the album every few months to capture your child's playing more advanced games and performing new actions that Baby couldn't undertake a few months earlier. In addition to making a terrific storybook that will help increase vocabulary, the photo album of Baby's friends will become a wonderful keepsake documenting your child's early years.

Create a memory game that features photos of your toddler, his friends, and his pets. Make two color copies for each photo you have. Cut color copies to fit onto fronts of old playing cards, then paste images onto the cards. To play the game, place all cards facedown on a table and ask your child to turn over two cards at a time. If he doesn't uncover two matching images, he must return the cards to a facedown position and keep uncovering two cards at a time until he makes a pair. This game sharpens memory skills and builds an understanding of pairs and matching like items.

Toddlers love to dress up in silly costumes and accessorize with bandannas, boas, scarves, wigs, hats, tiaras, wands, masks, and costume jewelry. Shop thrift stores and consignment shops for inexpensive, gently used Halloween costumes and fun dress-up clothes, then take photos of your child decked out in costumes that she's put together herself. Sit together and talk about each of the imaginary characters she's created, and encourage her to come up with a silly story for each photo or a thrilling tale that strings all of the characters together. Take careful notes, so that you can transcribe her story line into a scrapbook containing her character photos. She'll love reaching for a storybook that contains an exciting adventure straight from her imagination!

If you have a digital camera and computer with a color printer, you can create your own dictionary picture books of common vocabulary words. Although you don't need a digital camera to create these books, which simply feature photographs of common household items, a digital camera will prevent you from spending money on several rolls of film and save you the cost of getting the photos developed. Start by taking close-up photos of objects that suit a particular theme: fruits and vegetables; toys (rattles, blocks, dolls, teddy bears, and rubber duckies); articles of Baby's clothing (shirts, pants, bibs, dresses, and mittens); or household furniture (tables, chairs, couches, dressers, and beds). Download your digital images onto the computer, placing a few photos on each page of your document, and typing in the name of the items for each photo. Print out pages and mount them in a scrapbook that has sturdy, easy-to-turn pages. Create several picture books, each with a different theme, to reinforce the names of everyday objects for your child.

All About Me

For a wonderful keepsake that your child will love to look through again and again, take snapshots of your baby each day she turns a month older. Use a computer to create a personalized birthday sign that she can pose with each month (for example, "I'm four months old today!"). Include the date and your child's height and weight on the sign. Here's a great way to recycle one of the many free calendars you receive each year from local stores, gas

I'm **4** months old today!

stations, and realty agencies: cover the calendar's photo pages with colorful Con-Tact paper, affix your baby's photo to the Con-Tact–paper page that corresponds to that month, and decorate with markers, stickers, and glitter pens. Keep a record of Baby's firsts by filling them in on the calendar as they take place: her first tooth, first crawl, first words, first trip to the zoo, etc.

This is a great project to work on with an older sibling who's adjusting to life with a new baby in the house. Let the older child come up with decorating ideas for the calendar and give him the special task of tracking and recording Baby's firsts. In addition to teaching him about time periods (days, weeks, and months) and stages of infant development, it'll give you great one-on-one time together to tell funny and heartwarming stories about all of his own firsts.

Babies love to look in mirrors. Although he won't be able to figure out for quite some time why the baby in the mirror seems to move every time he does, his reflection is sure to elicit plenty of giggles and big smiles. Point to and identify parts of his face in the mirror, encourage him to razz or stick out his tongue at the baby in the mirror, or to wave and say "Hi" to his reflection. Hold him just out of visual range of the mirror and ask, "Where's Baby?" Then move him in front of the mirror and say, "Peekaboo! There's Baby!" Try out silly hats or talk to puppets and dolls in the mirror for added fun.

Tape-record your baby's coos, gurgles, and first words, then play them back to him to see his response. Some babies become animated and giggly when they hear their voice on tape, while others may respond with quiet fascination. Add to the tape periodically, announcing the date and Baby's age before each babbling session.

Toddlers love to hear their voices on tape and will be more than happy to supply you with hours of musical performances and comedy material for their recording sessions! Ask your child to sing favorite tunes, recite nursery rhymes, or just talk about the day's adventures. She'll love listening to the finished product and will probably sing along and converse with her recorded voice. Consider making your recording sessions a weekly ritual, adding each installment to the same cassette. Date your tapes and affix a color copy of a recent photo to each cassette cover. Tapes of your child's voice make precious family keepsakes.

Trace your toddler's full-body outline onto a piece of large poster board. Help him color in his hair, facial features, and clothing with crayons and markers. As you add details to his picture, discuss the color and texture of his hair and skin, the shape of his nose, the shape and color of his eyes, and any birthmarks or freckles he may have. Keep a mirror nearby to use as a visual reference. Once the picture is completed, use it to quiz him on the names of body parts, discuss the left and right sides of his body, and locate "body pairs," such as eyes, ears, arms, and legs.

Use a digital camera to take close-up shots of your child's face, arms, hands, legs, feet, and tummy for a lesson on body parts. With the aid of your computer, you can hone in on and isolate specific parts of your child's body. For example, you can zoom in on a digital scan of Baby's face, and cut out a nose, ear, eye, or mouth from that selected image and paste it into a computer document. Add typed captions for all of your close-up shots to create an *All About My Body* book. Point out specific body features in the book, name them for Baby, then show him these same features on you. You may also want to use a mirror to encourage him to locate his own body parts.

Introduce your child to common verbs and adjectives that will help her express herself. Cut out photos from parenting magazines of children playing, running, eating, and engaging in a variety of activities. Be sure to include close-up images of different facial expressions. Paste the cutout images in a scrapbook and create a story that utilizes an array of action words and phrases to describe emotions.

Create a growth chart to give your child a starting-off point for learning about foot and inch measurements. This long-term project also teaches budding scientists how to track progress and record results. Since a growth chart needs a permanent residence, you may want to think twice about locating it in your child's bedroom: years from now, she may frown upon the existence of a childhood chart in her teenage bedroom! Consider low-profile areas where you won't be entertaining guests, like a mudroom, laundry area, basement, or recreation room.

Once you've found the appropriate location, hot-glue a yardstick to the wall, ensuring that its bottom edge is flush with the floor and that the stick itself is level and straight on the wall. Use a permanent felt-tip pen to mark Baby's height, recording the date and his age next to the mark you've made. Children do the most growing during the first year, so record Baby's height each month. Since she won't be able to stand until eight to twelve months, use a tape measure to measure her length while lying down and transfer the measurement to the growth chart.

Once she's a toddler, you may choose to track her height every three months. For kindergartners and up, take yearly measurements. (Be sure to add another yardstick once she passes the 3-foot mark.) For a visual record of her growth, consider taking instant photos of your child posing with the growth chart, then mount the photos next to the corresponding growth chart entries.

"Handy" Games

Whether they're wiggling, clapping, or snapping, their hands and fingers provide an endless source of amusement for babies, and playing with them is an activity that will probably occupy many of their waking hours. Capitalize on this interest by helping your child discover the many amazing things he can do and learn with his hands.

Sing songs to help Baby discover the names of these very important body parts. Here are two that will come in handy:

"If you're happy and you know it, clap your hands.
If you're happy and you know it, clap your hands.
If you're happy and you know it,
then your face will surely show it.
If you're happy and you know it, clap your hands."

Pique Baby's curiosity by placing a ball or favorite toy in a tube sock or even placing it under his shirt. He will be intent in his determination to uncover the hidden object, concentrating all of his efforts on wriggling it back out. This is a good way for Baby to learn about the permanence of objects— they exist even when hidden.

Let your child create her very own masterpiece and sharpen her eye-hand coordination at the same time. Painting flat outdoor surfaces with water will occupy your child for hours (and the no-mess factor means *you* won't be occupied with cleaning when she's finished!). Provide your little one with paintbrushes in various sizes and a bowl of water. The darkened appearance of water painted on concrete walkways, tarred driveways, or wooden deck surfaces will seem magical to her.

Create homemade finger puppets with your toddler. Decorate the fingers of an old white or beige glove with silly faces, using felt-tipped pens. Create hats, bow ties, and animal ears with felt and fabric scraps. For quick and easy puppets, simply affix character stickers to each finger of the glove.

Here's a fun way for your child to become a puppet in her own show. As if making a mask for her, hold a paper plate up to your child's face to get an approximate idea of where to cut out eyeholes and a mouth. Once you've sketched them out, cut out the eyes and mouth area. Help her decorate the paper-plate faces to look like characters from her favorite storybook, fairy tale, or nursery rhyme. Add facial features with colorful markers, and glue on a wig, fabric fur, or dry macaroni for hair. Affix paper-plate faces to plastic rulers. Your child and her friends can maneuver the rulers so that the paper plates cover their faces when they are acting out the story.

Sock puppets are always a favorite with toddlers. If you don't have much luck finding anything other than stray white socks at your house, browse through thrift stores for socks in bright hues and patterns. Green socks are great for creating dragon, frog, and snake puppets. Use pink socks for pigs, yellow for ducks, and brown for monkeys, bears, or dogs. Find socks with animal patterns to create zebras, giraffes, tigers, and leopards for your toddler's next safari adventure. Once you've stocked—or socked!—up on the basics, start accessorizing: hot-glue fabric fur or yarn for hair, buttons for noses, and felt for eyes, ears, tongues, and bow ties.

Even cardboard toilet-paper tubes can make fun finger puppets. Hot-glue wiggly eyes, yarn hair, and felt accessories to your tube people. Place the finished tube over your toddler's middle and pointer fingers, which together will work to manipulate the puppet. Her thumb and ring finger can then function as arms for the puppet.

✦ Create a poster board of textures to help babies develop tactile discernment and practice fine motor skills, and to help strengthen toddlers' vocabulary acquisition as they link their sense of touch to sight and language. Track down plush carpet scraps, squishy sponges, crinkly cellophane, shiny aluminum foil, fur fabric, satin scarves, slick rain-jacket material, and rough sandpaper (that's been worn down to prevent scratching child's fingers). Securely hot-glue these items to a sturdy piece of poster board and let your child explore the different textures with her fingers. To give your toddler an idea of how these textures relate to real-world objects, create simple illustrations that incorporate the textures. For example, use the aluminum foil to make a bathroom mirror, glue the fur fabric onto an illustration of a dog, or paint an ocean scene and use sandpaper as your sandy beach. Ask for your child's input on how best to showcase the various textures, and she just may come up with a wonderful story line that incorporates all of the 3-D images.

Animal Adventures

Teach animal names and sounds, using animal crackers and the "Old MacDonald's Farm" song. Sit Baby in her high chair and spread out several animal crackers. As you sing about each animal, pick up the corresponding cracker and make it dance atop her food tray. It won't be long before she can pick out the corresponding cracker as soon as she hears you sing the animal's name.

Create a storybook with your toddler, using pictures of your pets. If you don't have pets, ask elementary-age cousins to send photos of their furry friends to your little one. Children love to write about animals, so invite them to enclose a special letter detailing how they feed and care for their pets. Help your child compose a letter to his cousins, thanking them for their pet stories and asking follow-up questions about their animals. For cousins who live far away from you, this is a great way to start a pen-pal correspondence that could last for years.

You don't need to spend a lot of money or travel too far from home to go on an animal adventure that will delight your kids. Even a simple field trip

to a nearby lake or forest can give them the opportunity to see and hear ducks, frogs, fish, squirrels, deer, and many interesting insects. Brush up on local animals with Baby Einstein's *Neighborhood Animals* book and see how many you can find on your field trip. To make it really feel like an adventure, bring along binoculars, a magnifying glass, a library book about regional wildlife, and a mini notebook for recording important animal findings and illustrations.

Fill up an inflatable kiddie pool with water and items to create your child's very own backyard pond. Add pond dwellers, like rubber duckies and plastic fish, turtles, dragonflies, and water bugs. Use green sponges to create floating lily pads for a few plastic frogs. Encourage your toddler to "quack," "ribbit," and "glub, glub" as he splashes about with his pond friends.

Enjoy a safari right in your own home, using stuffed animal and puppet monkeys, zebras, lions, tigers, and other exotic animals. Baby will love hearing you mimic the sounds of the animals as you put on a show for her, while your toddler will enjoy putting on a show for *you*. Expose your child to real-life images of these creatures in their natural habitats by incorporating the Baby Einstein Animal Discovery Cards into your game. To add another dimension to your safari adventure, check your local library's audio section for CDs or cassettes of jungle sounds.

Find out if there are any farms in your area that are open to the public. Aside from hearing the "oinks," "moos," and "neighs" of farm animals in person, your kids may even get the chance to see cows being milked, chickens laying eggs, pigs nursing a litter of piglets, and horses being groomed.

Nurturing With Nature

Baby will love exploring the many textures, colors, and scents your yard has to offer. Discover the uplifting scents and exciting textures of pine needles and pinecones. Tickle him with blades of grass and let him experience the thrill of crawling over a cool lawn and taking in its fresh scent. Point out squirrels, crows, and birds, and imitate their sounds. Take a few moments to absorb all that your property has to offer; rediscover it through your baby's eyes and consider the many science lessons it can provide about your region's animals, plants, and climate in the months to come.

Discover silly noises you can make with items found in nature. Bite into an apple or jump into a pile of leaves to let Baby hear what "crunch" sounds like. Make a blade of wet grass "squeak" or pebbles "plunk" into a brook. Listen to the wind "swoosh" and the rain go "pitter-patter." Take a walk in the backyard or in your neighborhood to find unique sounds that will make your baby giggle.

Here's a novel idea for a rainy-day adventure—go outside! Take your umbrellas and galoshes out during a light rain for a unique, multisensory experience. Encourage your child to feel the rain on his hands and face, and catch raindrops in his mouth. Listen to the gentle pitter-patter on your umbrella; spin your umbrellas around and hear the different effects the rain makes at varying speeds. If you don't mind the mess, splash around in puddles and talk about the sounds you make. Look for common rainy-day creatures, such as slugs, worms, and toads. Warm up by spending the rest of your rainy day at the library to find out more about these newfound friends.

Children are natural collectors and—*naturally*—love to collect items from nature! Take them on an outdoor adventure, whether it be to a popular hiking site, a simple wooded area in your town, or even your backyard. Bring a basket to collect unusual flowers, attractive leaves, and interesting nuts and seeds. Once home, use a plant or flower press to preserve the collection. Check out a

 few field guides from the local library—older children will especially love to play detective, tracking down clues about the "unidentified suspects" in their collection. Once identified, they may want to glue their pressed naturals into a nature walk scrapbook or onto construction paper to create a one-of-a-kind wall hanging for their room.

⭐ Ask friends and family members across the country to send scenic postcards representative of their hometowns, with messages about what their neighborhood and climate is like and about the plants, animals, and insects that inhabit their neck of the woods. Place postcards in a photo album with sleeves that allow you to see the backs and fronts of the cards when you turn the pages of your neighborhoods-around-the-country storybook.

⭐ Visiting local garden centers and botanical gardens is a wonderful way to expose your child to the sights, smells, and textures of flowers, herbs, and shrubs. Make a game out of finding shapes on plants (such as heart-shaped lilacs, star-shaped columbines, and oval basil leaves) or ask them to track down plants representing every color in the rainbow (such as red roses, orange lilies, yellow daffodils, green hostas, blue hydrangeas, purple irises, and pink snapdragons).

Shaping Up

Keep Baby occupied as he gets his diaper changed by hanging a mobile of plastic cookie cutters over his changing area. If his changing table is near a window, simply suspend a plastic hanger from the curtain rod, using plastic chain links. Add cookie cutters to the base of the hanger, using more links. When Baby starts getting fussy, simply distract him by pointing out the star, circle, heart, and triangle shapes dancing overhead.

Introduce Baby to everyday shapes, using common household items. Collect round balls, oval place mats, square books, triangular plastic hangers, empty rectangular tissue boxes, and heart-shaped lids from candy containers. Place these items in a plastic storage box, talking about the shape of each, and ask your child to pick out the shape as you call it out. Carry her with you and go from room to room, pointing out the many shapes that surround her.

It's easy for children to get antsy when sitting down to eat, so keep fussiness to a minimum by serving up a meal of shapes! Just before mealtime, ask your child to help you find an array of edible shapes in your kitchen, such as oval hard-boiled eggs, round tomato slices, triangular tortilla chips, crescent-shaped bananas, square cheese slices, and rectangular graham crackers. Your child will enjoy the sense of independence she gains from picking out her own menu (and will probably stay seated at the table until she's finished her meal!). When you run out of ideas for finding already existing food shapes, simply make your own shapely creations with cookie cutters: create circular sandwiches, heart-shaped ham slices, and star-shaped apple slices.

Make a shape sorter, using a shoe box and cookie cutters. Use a pencil to trace around plastic cookie cutters you've positioned on the box lid; cut out shapes with a utility knife, then replace the lid on the box. Your child will spend hours fitting the cookie cutters into the holes, removing the lid to shake out the cutters, and then replacing the lid to start the game all over again.

Exploring Math and Science

Playing with spinning toys builds coordination, aids in sensory motor development, and sets the stage for scientific exploration—so take one for a spin! Make your own spinning top with poster board, a plastic coffee-can lid, and a skewer stick. Trace around the lid on the poster board and cut out a circle. Paint a swirling spiral or other whimsical design onto the poster board circle. Alternatively, decorate with magazine cutouts of baby faces or even color-copied cutouts of your own baby's face. Use a nail to poke a hole through the poster board and lid. Slide a blunt-edged chopstick through both holes, and you're ready to start spinning. Watch your baby's reaction to the top spinning before him: his gaze will be fixed on the mesmerizing color in motion.

 Puzzles are great tools for demonstrating how smaller parts fit together to create a whole. Color-copy a favorite photo of your child or pet, enlarging it to fit the size of a standard paper plate. Use a pencil to trace around plate onto color-copied image, centering the image as desired, then cut out image and mount it on the paper plate. Cut the paper plate into four or five pieces. Mix up the pieces and show Baby how they fit together to make a complete picture.

Find whimsical plastic children's place mats at thrift shops and garage sales and cut them up into several large pieces. These make great toys to keep kids busy while waiting at the doctor's office and can be easily transported in a resealable plastic bag. Once your kids have mastered piecing together individual place-mat puzzles, put the pieces of two or three different puzzles into the same plastic bag; they'll enjoy the challenge of sorting and matching up the mixed-up pieces.

Teach Baby about opposites by demonstrating how things work around the house: the light switch goes on and off, doors let you go in and out of the house, dresser drawers open and close, running water can be warm or cold, drinking glasses can be empty or full, and sweatshirt zippers pull up and down, while suitcase zippers move left to right.

Fill an empty paper milk carton with water and drop in favorite plastic toys. Freeze, then peel off the paper carton to reveal a frozen block of toys. Let your child see and touch the cold block and discuss how it feels and what she sees. Place the block in a sink to watch the ice melt in hot water and magically release her toys. This scientific exercise will introduce her to the liquid, frozen, and gas states of water.

Future architects will love constructing forts and playhouses from large cardboard boxes—a good exercise in spatial relationships. Call around and see if local appliance stores, electronic outlets, or home-supply stores have any large boxes you could take off their hands. Use a utility knife to fashion a front door that's just your toddler's size and add a few windows. Sit down

with your toddler to discuss your construction plans. Where does he want to put the house? Is it for indoor or outdoor play? What would he like his cardboard house to look like on the outside? What would he like to put inside the house? How many boxes will you need to tape together to create the house he's envisioning? Your toddler will love offering his input and insights and will gain confidence in his decision-making skills. You may want to suggest different ways to cover or decorate the box's exterior (using construction paper, wrapping paper, favorite stickers, or trading cards), as well as fun ideas for decorating inside (towels for curtains, beanbag chairs, transistor radio, small table, a battery-operated camping lamp, and glow-in-the dark stars on the walls).

⭐ Stir up some magic right in your kitchen with an easy-to-make bubble-blowing solution. Mix together 1/2 cup water with a tablespoon of dishwashing liquid (do not use laundry detergent or detergent designed for a dishwasher, as they are toxic). For bubble wands, experiment with funnels, slotted spoons, and potato mashers for different results.

Color Their Worlds

Many game spinners from children's board games feature bright colors or numbers on their faces. Although Baby is too young to enjoy a board game, a game spinner to help her learn the names of colors and numbers may be just her speed! To play with these "spinning flash cards," simply spin the arrow and call out the number or color the arrow lands on.

Encourage your child to come up with his own rhymes and songs about colors and sounds. Use "rattle jars" to reinforce the names of colors. Find as many jars as needed to represent each color found in a package of construction paper. Selecting a different color for each jar, roll up a piece of construction paper (cut to fit height of jar) and place it inside so that it covers the sides of the glass. Place different noisemakers, like rattles, large jingle bells, or keys, in each jar. Then play musical color games with your rainbow of rattle jars: "Pick up the big blue jar and shake it, shake it, near and far."

Find a bunch of solid-colored chiffon scarves or lightweight pieces of fabric that will float when thrown up in the air. As you throw them in the air to float down to Baby, name the scarf's color: "Whee! There's a BLUE scarf that's flying way up high. It's floating down to Michael. You can catch it if you try!" Play peekaboo with each scarf, reinforcing the names of colors: "Where's Julia? Is she hiding under the RED scarf? Peekaboo!"

Here's a great game to play when stuck inside on a rainy day. Select a crayon and scribble a patch of color on the page of a miniature notebook. Send your child on a colorful fact-finding mission, asking him to find as many items as he can in the house that match the color scribbled on his notebook page.

Serve food with a color theme to add some excitement to mealtime and learn about colors, bite by bite. Try a yellow breakfast, featuring scrambled eggs, apple juice, bananas, and melted cheese on a potato-bread slice. Enjoy a red lunch of spaghetti with tomato sauce, beets, cranberry juice, and sliced strawberries and raspberries. For dinner, you can even make the color brown exciting: meat loaf, baked potato, gravy, sautéed mushrooms, Bosc pears, chocolate milk, and gingerbread cookies for dessert.

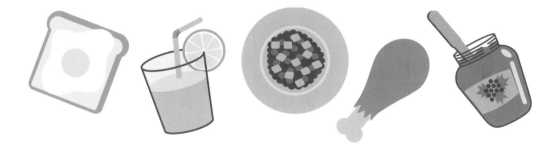

Music to Their Ears

You can make homemade rattles, using yogurt containers, plastic water or juice bottles, and small, plastic kitchen containers. Fill containers with household items that are sure to clank and rattle: rice, shells, dried beans, popcorn kernels, candy sprinkles, or large wooden spools. Ensure that container lids are securely fastened for Baby's safety, then shake rattle to this song:

> **"Shake, shake! What a fun sound.**
> **I love to shake my rattle around!"**

Encourage Baby to shake the rattle herself.

Create a rattle that's also fun to cuddle. Remove the stuffing from a small stuffed animal. Replace stuffing with keys, then sew the toy shut. For crinkly rattles, fill stuffed toys with cellophane paper.

Baby will love discovering the different effects he can create by experimenting with a range of homemade drumsticks. Help him create his own beat with plastic spatulas, measuring spoons, plastic pail shovels, or toy xylophone mallets. For the baby who hasn't yet graduated to solid foods, here's a great way to ease his transition into the high chair: sit him in the high chair every day with his drumsticks and let him bang out a tune on the food tray.

Try to stump your kids with the "Guess the Sound" game. Cover a jar with construction paper and ask them to close their eyes as you put a mystery item inside. Shake the jar and have them guess just what it is you're shaking inside your jar. If they're stumped, give them subtle clues to help solve the mystery: "This is something you use to eat cereal. It has a long handle." Consider shaking a set of keys, metal measuring spoons, dried rice, large wooden spools, and other household items you can find "rattling around" in your pantry or junk drawers. Be sure to utilize items that won't pose choking hazards.

Toddlers will love keeping time to music with their very own set of maracas made from a potato-chip canister. Fill the canister halfway with rice or dried beans; replace the plastic lid and secure it with a strip of masking tape. Cover the canister with construction paper and let your child decorate the exterior with markers and crayons.

 Turn empty, cylinder-shaped oatmeal boxes or empty coffee cans into a set of bongo drums. Hot-glue a long wooden spool between two of the boxes to create your bongo set. Decorate the drums with markers and crayons.

Mouth instruments will help your child learn how to maneuver her lips and tongue when taking measured breaths to blow out air. This is good practice for speech development. Cover one end of a cardboard toilet-paper roll with waxed paper; secure the paper with hot glue. Take turns making a "doo-doo-doo" kazoo sound into the open end. Try out favorite words, animal sounds, and silly songs with the kazoo. Your child will love to feel the words tickle her mouth as the sound reverberates in the tube. She will also enjoy tooting her horn through a plastic kitchen funnel or even into a disposable plastic cup. The amplified sounds she creates will provide endless amusement.

Discover the do-it-yourself drum corps that's hidden in your kitchen cabinets. March out those pots, pans, pie tins, empty cereal boxes, metal measuring cups, plastic mixing bowls, cookie sheets, and plastic pitchers for some percussive playtime. Empty formula canisters make great percussion instruments, providing a sturdy plastic drumming surface as well as a metal bottom for a steel drum sound. Sing this song as you drum together:

> *"Bum-dee-dee-bum, Billy's in a band.*
> *He can play the drums with his hands.*
> *Bum-dee-dee-bum, Billy's having fun—*
> *Drumming with those fingers and thumbs!"*

Seasonal Fun

Create paper snowflakes, using colorful metallic papers and glitter pens. Attach sparkly snowflakes to car windows out of Baby's reach to occupy him while he's in his car seat. Or dangle them from a plastic hanger to create a lovely winter mobile for him to gaze at in his room. Ensure that the mobile is positioned far out of Baby's reach. Consider updating the mobile each season: flowers for spring, smiling suns for summer, and colorful leaves for autumn.

Children are captivated by the touch, taste, and sight of snow, and all the magic that winter has to offer. If you don't live in a climate with cold winters, create your own "snow" in the bathtub with crushed ice—it's a great way for Baby to learn about the word "cold" and an opportunity for him to explore a new, slushy texture.

Add several drops of food coloring to a spray bottle of water and paint the snow outside with fun stars, smiley faces, numbers, letters, triangles, and other fun designs.

In autumn, go on a leaf hunt with your toddler. Collect an array of brilliant red, orange, and yellow leaves in different shapes and sizes. Arrange your child's collection between two sheets of waxed paper. Place a dish towel on top of the waxed paper and, using a warm setting, iron the towel on a warm setting to preserve the leaves. After you identify the leaves and learn a bit about the trees they came from, display the preserved leaves on your windows as fun, seasonal decorations or in picture frames to give as gifts or to decorate your child's bedroom.

Instead of buying one large Halloween pumpkin for your child to decorate, purchase several minigourds and give each one a different expression. Talk about the different faces she wants to create, such as happy, spooky, silly, sad, and scared ones. Sketch out her ideas on paper, giving thoughtful consideration to the shape of the gourd (round, hourglass, square, or oval) and how it will add to the effect she wants to create. Since carving is a lot of messy work and doesn't allow kids hands-on involvement, use markers, glitter pens, hats, and Halloween costume accessories to dress up your gourds instead.

It's easy to make your own snow globes, using large-sized baby food jars with tight-fitting lids. Use epoxy glue (or another waterproof glue) to adhere a plastic figurine to the inside of the jar lid. Let glue dry completely. Fill jar almost to top with distilled water, adding a drop or two of glycerine or baby oil. Add a pinch or two of white or silver glitter to create "snow," then permanently fasten the lid to the jar, turn it upside down, and enjoy the snowy scene. Homemade snow globes make wonderful stocking stuffers.

Enjoy a snowy treat on a summer day: Make snow cones with crushed ice and your child's favorite juice, for a treat that is not only tasty to toddlers but is also comforting to teething babies.

Create a holiday storybook starring your family. Older children can help you write text to accompany photos of your kids playing in the snow, sitting on Santa's lap, eating holiday cookies, wrapping presents, and decorating the Christmas tree.

Sure to become a treasured family keepsake, this special storybook will be something your kids will look forward to reading every holiday season, no matter how old they are.

Learn More at the Store

Turn an everyday trip to the grocery store into a magical learning experience. The produce aisle is ideal for exposing Baby to colors (red apples and yellow lemons), textures (rough coconuts and fuzzy kiwis), and shapes (round oranges and crescent-shaped bananas). As you check out your store's fresh and steaming soup selections, expose Baby to "warm" words, then stroll to the frozen-foods aisles for a "cool" lesson.

Keep toddlers entertained on shopping trips by letting them track down many of the items on your grocery list. Write out your list, using large, easy-to-read words. Point to the words as you request the items, and bring along a pen so that your child can cross off the items as he finds them.

If you're really ambitious, turn your shopping list into a bingo grid and let him draw an "X" through each grid square as he finds a listed item listed. Reward your child's assistance by writing "Special Treat for Me" inside the center square—for instance, a free pass to select one toy or treat of his choice from the store. This is a great way to stress independent thinking and teach decision-making. Sticking to a specific list and offering a special reward at the end of your trip will keep your child engaged and prevent numerous requests (and demanding cries) for the multitude of enticing snacks on the store shelves as you shop!

⭐ Reinforce the words you just learned at the store by naming items for Baby as you unload your grocery bags or by asking your toddler to unpack groceries with you and name each item he pulls out. Figuring out where all of the items go in your home is a great problem-solving exercise that sharpens sorting and matching skills.

SQUARE   RED   COLD

chapter 3

Tools for Learning

This chapter provides everything you need to take Baby on a visual and aural exploration of the fine arts—a magical journey that is certain to promote a lifetime love of learning. And there is no better guide for this learning expedition than a caring parent. Designed to support and encourage dynamic interaction between parent and child, this section contains a carefully selected listing of poetry anthologies, classical music, and books featuring great masterpieces. These baby-friendly educational resources will invite your child to discover the greatest forms of human expression—language, poetry, music, and art.

Exposure to the fine arts will expand your child's emotional and intellectual comprehension of words, music, and images. Reading poetry and rhymes to children enhances vocabulary acquisition, promotes speech development, and helps develop a keen sense of language patterns. Through fine works of art, the varied shapes, colors, and emotions of "the world at large" become accessible to children, while the beneficial effects of listening to classical music (including the acquisition of memory and verbal skills and spatial reasoning abilities) are innumerable. Find special ways to incorporate the humanities into Baby's daily routine: in the morning, explore Marc Chagall's vivid colors and whimsical creatures to awaken the senses; set the stage for imaginative playtime in the afternoon with rollicking Bach melodies; and then cuddle together to read Robert Louis Stevenson's *A Child's Garden of Verse* for classic childhood poems that are sure to inspire wondrous bedtime dreams.

Baby-Friendly Poetry Anthologies

Animal Crackers: A Delectable Collection of Pictures, Poems, and Lullabies for the Very Young
Jane Dyer (editor). Boston: Little, Brown and Company, 1996.

*Popular rhymes, lullabies, classic poems, and contemporary verses about counting, ABCs, shapes, colors, seasons, and animals are richly framed by Dyer's dazzling watercolor illustrations.

Around the World in Eighty Poems
James Berry (editor). San Francisco: Chronicle Books, 2002.

*This book takes an imaginary journey around the world using poems from more than fifty different countries, including Greenland, Kenya, Greece, South Africa, and Ireland.

The Beauty of the Beast: Poems from the Animal Kingdom

Jack Prelutsky (editor). New York: Alfred A. Knopf; distributed by Random House, 1997.

*An illustrated collection of more than 200 animal poems, including verses by Maurice Sendak, Carl Sandburg, and Ogden Nash, which are conveniently classified into five sections: insects, fish, reptiles, birds, and mammals.

A Child's Garden of Verses

Robert Louis Stevenson. New York: Simon & Schuster Books for Young Readers, 1999.

*First published in 1885, this classic treasury of Stevenson's poems, accompanied in this edition by Tasha Tudor's richly hued watercolors, paints a timeless, intimate portrait of the bliss and wonder of childhood.

Climb Into My Lap: First Poems to Read Together

Lee Bennett Hopkins (editor). New York: Simon & Schuster Books for Young Readers, 1998.

*From story poems, and rhymes for finger play, to verses about magical fairy worlds and "secret places," this anthology combines beloved poets with new voices.

Color Me a Rhyme: Nature Poems for Young People

Jane Yolen. Honesdale, Penn.: Wordsong Boyd Mills Press, 2000.

*A poem for every color of the rainbow, accompanied by striking photographs from nature and famous quotes about color.

Eloise Wilkin's Poems to Read to the Very Young

Josette Frank (editor). New York: Random House, 1982.

*Accompanying uplifting poetry by Christina Rossetti, Sarah Coleridge, Kate Greenaway, and other classic poets, Wilkin's stunning illustrations, which have delighted generations of youngsters, capture the innocence and euphoria of childhood.

Fingerplays and Songs for the Very Young

Carolyn Croll (illustrator). New York: Random House, 2001.

*This sturdy board book contains more than twenty-five action songs (like "The Wheels on the Bus" and "Ride a Horse to Boston") and rhymes for finger games (like "Five Little Monkeys" and "Open, Shut Them!") that are sure to elicit big giggles from babies and toddlers.

Good Night, Sleep Tight:
A Poem for Every Night of the Year

Ivan and Mal Jones (editors). New York: Scholastic Trade, 2000.

*This collection of 366 bedtime poems for every night of the year (including February 29!) features selections by William Shakespeare, William Blake, Eugene Field, and Eve Merriam, along with poems by children and folk rhymes from around the world.

Grassroots: Poems by Carl Sandburg

Carl Sandburg. San Diego: Harcourt Brace & Company, 1998.

*Set against nostalgic illustrations of farms, prairies, and majestic fields are fourteen timeless poems that pay tribute to the sights, sounds, textures, and people of the Midwest.

Kay Chorao's Big Book for Babies

Kay Chorao (editor). New York: Barnes & Noble Books, 1998.

*Collected in one volume are three of Chorao's beautifully illustrated poetry anthologies— *Baby's Good Morning Book*, *Baby's Lap Book*, and *Baby's Bedtime Book*—providing Baby with jaunty "rise and shine" poems from A. A. Milne and Rose Fyleman, midday story time with treasured nursery rhymes from the *Lap Book*, and lulling *Bedtime Book* poems by such writers as Tennyson and Blake.

My First Oxford Book of Poems

John Foster (editor). New York: Oxford University Press, 2001.

*This anthology of eighty-eight best-loved traditional and modern poems is thematically grouped according to subject matter: nature, animals, the sea, bedtime, weather and seasons, and the "fantastical and nonsensical."

My Very First Mother Goose

Iona Opie (editor). Cambridge, Massachusetts: Candlewick Press, 1996.

*This collection contains more than sixty nursery rhymes, including "Pussycat, Pussycat," "Hey, Diddle, Diddle," and "Pat-a-Cake," with beautiful artwork by popular children's illustrator Rosemary Wells.

Poems for the Very Young

Michael Rosen (editor). New York: Kingfisher Books, 1993.

*A varied selection of modern and traditional poems from different parts of the world, each with rhythmic, playful qualities that make reading aloud especially enjoyable.

Poetry for Young People: Edward Lear

Edward Mendelson (editor). New York: Sterling Publishing Company, Inc., 2001.

*This treasury of thirty-five amusing poems and limericks will amuse with silly, nonsense words like "Scroobius Pip" and its host of charming and mischievous characters.

Pretty Poems and Wonderful Words

Baby Einstein. Julie Aigner-Clark. New York: Hyperion Books for Children, 2003.

*This charmingly illustrated book with lift-the-flap surprises features classic poems of Robert Louis Stevenson.

The Random House Book of Poetry for Children

Jack Prelutsky (editor). New York: Random House, 1983.

*This comprehensive anthology contains more than 550 poems, silly verses, and playground chants by American, English, and anonymous contributors.

The Read-Aloud Treasury: Favorite Nursery Rhymes, Poems, Stories, and More for the Very Young

Joanna Cole, Stephanie Calmenson (editors). New York: Doubleday, 1988.

*In addition to Mother Goose favorites and works by renowned poets such as Edward Lear, A. A. Milne, and Robert Louis Stevenson, this treasury also contains classic stories like "Goldilocks" and "Gingerbread Man," and a Play and Learn section featuring rebus stories and seek-and-find games.

Ride a Purple Pelican

Jack Prelutsky. New York: Greenwillow Books, 1986.

*Garth Williams's fanciful illustrations bring the silly characters of these enchanting, nonsensical nursery rhymes to life.

Stopping by Woods on a Snowy Evening

Robert Frost. New York: Dutton Children's Books, 1978.

*Illustrator Susan Jeffers brings each verse of Frost's beloved poem to life with stunning artwork that perfectly captures the quiet beauty of a frosty New England evening.

The Sweet and Sour Animal Book

Langston Hughes. New York: Oxford University Press, 1994.

*From "Ape" to "Zebra," short and clever poems take children through both the alphabet and the animal world.

Talking Like the Rain: A Read-to-Me Book of Poems

X. J. Kennedy, Dorothy M. Kennedy (editors). Boston: Little, Brown & Company, 1992.

*More than 100 poems featuring notables such as Emily Dickinson, Ogden Nash, Robert Frost, and Langston Hughes delight in the joys of childhood both in words and in watercolor images rendered by Jane Dyer.

Under Water with Ogden Nash

Ogden Nash. Boston: Little, Brown and Company, 1997.

*Twenty-seven of Nash's playful, nonsensical rhymes about aquatic creatures, from hippos and swans to sharks and mermaids, are beautifully illustrated by botanical and zoological illustrator Katie Lee.

Where the Sidewalk Ends: The Poems & Drawings of Shel Silverstein

Shel Silverstein. New York: HarperCollins Juvenile Books, 1974.

*This collection of 130 poems, which range from touching and poignant to silly and laugh-out-loud preposterous, is sure to tickle your toddler's funny bone and instill a genuine love for poetry.

Winter Poems

Barbara Rogasky (editor). New York: Scholastic, Inc., 1994.

*Classic poems by Sara Teasdale, Edna St. Vincent Millay, William Shakespeare, William Wordsworth, and other notables commemorate the thrills and chills of the winter season.

A Year Full of Poems

Michael Hansen, Christopher Stuart-Clark (editors). New York: Oxford University Press, 1991.

*With verses celebrating the sights and sounds of each season, this book's unique January-through-December format features eight to twelve poems, including works by Emily Bronte, D. H. Lawrence, and Sara Teasdale, which capture the true essence of each month.

Baby-Friendly Art Books

The ABCs of Art

Baby Einstein. Julie Aigner-Clark, New York: Hyperion Books for Children, 2002.

*Each letter of the alphabet is introduced to children through photographs of famous works of art from Van Gogh to Warhol. In addition to learning the alphabet, children will develop a lifelong love of art.

A is for Artist: A Getty Museum Alphabet

J. Paul Getty Museum, John Harris (editor). Los Angeles: J. Paul Getty Museum, 1997.

*"A is for artist," "B is for bumblebee," and "C is for candle" in this lovely alphabet book that encourages children to closely examine twenty-six masterpieces by various artists, including Vincent van Gogh, Paul Cézanne, and Edgar Degas, in search of the objects or images that represent each letter of the alphabet.

A Child's Book of Art: Great Pictures, First Words

Lucy Micklethwait. New York: DK Publishing, 1993.

*With thematic, baby-friendly categories such as shapes, opposites, counting, colors, action words, and animals on the farm, this book utilizes great masterpieces to illustrate simple vocabulary words.

A Child's Book of Lullabies

Shona McKellar (editor), Mary Cassatt (illustrator). New York: DK Publishing, 1997.

*The sweet sentiments expressed in "Sleep, Baby, Sleep," "Sweet and Low," "Twinkle, Twinkle, Little Star," and other cherished lullabies are lovingly echoed in Mary Cassatt's warm, intimate paintings of mothers with their children.

Come Look with Me: World of Play

Gladys S. Blizzard. Charlottesville, Virginia: Thomasson-Grant, Inc., 1993.

*This collection of twelve works of art features people at play with thought-provoking questions for older children that can be easily tailored to suit toddler level.

Curious Cats: In Art and Poetry

Metropolitan Museum of Art, William Lach (editor). New York: Atheneum Books for Young Readers, an imprint of Simon & Schuster, 1999.

*Cat poems, limericks, haiku, and nursery rhymes—by such notables as T. S. Eliot, Emily Dickinson, and Langston Hughes—are paired with their artful feline counterparts in works by Toulouse-Lautrec, Goya, Currier & Ives, and artists from around the world.

How Artists See Families: Mother, Father, Sister, Brother

Colleen Carroll. New York: Abbeville Kids, 1997.

*Here's a fascinating look at how families have been portrayed in fine art from different time periods and places, along with thought-provoking questions to start your own family discussions.

I Dreamed I Was a Ballerina

Anna Pavlova, Edgar Degas (illustrator). New York: Atheneum Books for Young Readers, an imprint of Simon & Schuster, 2001.

*Breathtaking pastels and paintings of ballerinas from the Metropolitan Museum of Art's Edgar Degas collection spin magic, awe, and inspiration into this simple tale drawn from the memoirs of the famous twentieth-century ballerina Anna Pavlova.

I Spy a Freight Train: Transportation in Art

Lucy Micklethwait. New York: Greenwillow Books, 1996.

*Showcasing paintings of artists such as Dali, Kandinsky, and van Gogh, this book invites readers to find a mode of transportation—such as a train, rowboat, wagon, or camel—in each work of art.

I Spy a Lion: Animals in Art

Lucy Micklethwait. New York: Greenwillow Books, 1994.

*Children will enjoy scanning famous works of art to uncover snakes, monkeys, mice, and other exciting creatures "hidden" in this interactive art-appreciation book.

I Spy: An Alphabet in Art

Lucy Micklethwait. New York: Greenwillow Books, 1991.

*This interactive book prompts toddlers to play the "I spy with my little eye" game with twenty-six timeless works of art, each containing an easy-to-find, everyday item that begins with a letter of the alphabet (like an apple for the letter "A" in Magritte's *Son of Man*).

Imaginary Gardens: American Poetry & Art for Young People

Charles Sullivan (editor). New York: Henry N. Abrams, Inc., 1989.

*Some of the most unlikely pairings of writers and artists, such as T. S. Eliot and Roy Lichtenstein, or Robert Frost and Keith Haring, make for perfect partners in this American art and poetry collection that will fascinate children and adults alike.

Lullabies: An Illustrated Songbook

Metropolitan Museum of Art, Richard Kapp (arranger). New York: Gulliver Books, 1997.

*Words and music for thirty-seven enchanting lullabies are thoughtfully paired with paintings by van Gogh, Cassatt, Manet, and other fine artists from the Metropolitan Museum of Art collection.

Museum ABC

Metropolitan Museum of Art. Boston: Little, Brown and Company, 2002.

*Each spread in this book contains an alphabet letter and a word beginning with that letter ("A is for apple") and four contrasting visual representations of that word to demonstrate how objects can be both the same and different in the eyes of various artists, cultures, and time periods.

1 to 10 and Back Again: A Getty Museum Counting Book

J. Paul Getty Museum. Los Angeles: J. Paul Getty Museum, 1998

*Opulent objects from the J. Paul Getty Museum's French Decorative Arts collection, such as gilded chairs, fine clocks, ornate teacups, and elaborate globes, offer a unique and visually stimulating approach to counting the numbers 1 to 10 forward and backward (and in English and in French).

Roy Lichtenstein's ABCs

Bob Adelman. Boston: Little, Brown & Company, 1999.

*The ABCs receive a pop-art makeover in this book of Lichtenstein prints, drawings, and paintings specifically selected for their alphabet-inspired images, like 1965's *Grrrrrrrrrrr!!*, which features a growling comic-book style dog for the letter "D."

Spot a Cat: A Child's Book of Art and Fun

Lucy Micklewait. New York: DK Publishing, 1995.

*Thirteen paintings from artists around the world challenge young minds to find the "big cat," "little cat," "happy cat," and other playful felines in each work of art, offering a dynamic "hide-and-seek" approach to art appreciation.

Spot a Dog: A Child's Book of Art and Fun

Lucy Micklewait. New York: DK Publishing, 1995.

*A companion to *Spot a Cat*, this book playfully invites children's eyes to frolic and roam through thirteen paintings, each containing a hidden dog.

Where's the Bear?: A Look-and-Find Book

J. Paul Getty Museum. Los Angeles: J. Paul Getty Museum, 1997.

*Twenty-five detailed close-ups of animals featured in Jan Brueghel's 1613 painting, *The Entry of the Animals into Noah's Ark,* grace the pages of this beautiful book, which provides the phonetic spelling for each animal in English, French, Spanish, German, Italian, and Japanese, along with a color foldout of the painting in its entirety.

Baby-Friendly Classical Music

Morning Melodies

"Allegro for a Flute Clock," Ludwig van Beethoven

Arabesque no. 1, Claude Debussy

"Arabian Dance (from *Peer Gynt*)," Edvard Grieg

"Arrival of the Queen of Sheba" (*Solomon*), George Frideric Handel

Etude in G-flat, Opus 10, no. 5 ("Black Keys"), Frédéric Chopin

"Images: Nocturnes for Orchestra" ("Sirènes"), Claude Debussy

"Liebesbotschaft" ("Message of Love"), Franz Liszt

"The Maiden's Wish," Franz Liszt

The Nutcracker Suite: "Dance of the Reed-pipes," Peter Ilyich Tchaikovsky

"Petit Suite—En Bateau," Claude Debussy

Prelude in G, Opus 28, no. 3, Frédéric Chopin

The Sleeping Beauty: "Panorama" (Act II), Peter Ilyich Tchaikovsky

Sonata in C major, KV 309 (*Allegro con spirito*), Wolfgang Amadeus Mozart

String Quartet no. 13 in B-flat, Op. 130 (*Alla danza tedesca, Allegro assai*), Ludwig van Beethoven

Symphony no. 33 in B-flat (*Allegro assai*), Wolfgang Amadeus Mozart

Bath-Time Music

Aria from *The Marriage of Figaro* ("Non Più Andrai"), Wolfgang Amadeus Mozart

"Brandenburg Concerto" no. 4, BWV 1049 (first movement), Johann Sebastian Bach

Contradance no. 5, Ludwig van Beethoven

Flute Concerto no. 4 in G (*Largo*), Antonio Vivaldi

Flute Sonata in Eb, BWV 1031 (first movement), Johann Sebastian Bach

Piano Sonata in A Major, K. 331 (*Andante gransioso*), Wolfgang Amadeus Mozart

"Deh Vieni alla Finestra," from *Don Giovanni,* K. 527, Wolfgang Amadeus Mozart

"Jeptha: Sinfonia," George Frideric Handel

"Les Jeux D'Eaux À La Villa D'Este," Franz Liszt

The Nutcracker Suite: "Dance of the Sugar Plum Fairy," Peter Ilyich Tchaikovsky

Piano Sonata no. 7 in D, Op. 10, no. 3—"Menuetto" (*Allegro*), Ludwig van Beethoven

Piano Sonata no. 15 in D, Op. 28 ("Pastoral")—Rondo (Allegro ma non troppo), Ludwig van Beethoven

Rondo in C, Op. 51, no. 1, Ludwig van Beethoven

Swan Lake: "Odette and the Prince" (Act II), Peter Ilyich Tchaikovsky

Violin Concerto no. 4 in D Major, K. 218 ("Rondeau"), Wolfgang Amadeus Mozart

Songs for Playtime or Dancing

The Bartered Bride, "Overture," Bedrich Smetana

The Bartered Bride, "Skocna," Bedrich Smetana

"Brandenburg Concerto" no. 5, BWV 1050 (3rd movement), Johann Sebastian Bach

"Clair de Lune," Claude Debussy

Contradance no. 4, Ludwig van Beethoven

"Goldberg Variations," no. 1, BWV 988, Johann Sebastian Bach

"Hall of the Mountain King" (from *Peer Gynt*), Edvard Grieg

The Creatures of Prometheus, Finale (*Allegretto*), Ludwig van Beethoven

The Marriage of Figaro, Overture, Wolfgang Amadeus Mozart

Military March no. 1 in F, WoO 18, Ludwig van Beethoven

Piano Sonata no. 11, K. 331 ("Rondo alla turca"—"Turkish March"), Wolfgang Amadeus Mozart

Piano Sonata no. 15, K. 545 (*Allegro*), Wolfgang Amadeus Mozart

Rondo a Capriccio in G, Op. 129, Ludwig van Beethoven

The Ruins of Athens, "Turkish March," Op. 113, Ludwig van Beethoven

Symphony no. 4, "Italian," Felix Mendelssohn

Symphony no. 8 in F, Op. 93 (*Allegro scherzando*), Ludwig van Beethoven

Tunes for Massage Time and Winding Down

"Eine Kleine Nachtmusik" ("Romance"), Wolfgang Amadeus Mozart

"Für Elise," Ludwig van Beethoven

"Grande Polonaise Brillante," Op. 22 (*Andante spianato: tranquillo*), Frédéric Chopin

"Jesu, Joy of Man's Desiring," BWV 147, Johann Sebastian Bach

"Liebestraum" ("Dream of Love"), Franz Liszt

"My Darling," Franz Lizst

Oboe Concerto in D Minor (*Adagio*), Thomas Albinoni

"Pastoral Symphony" (*Messiah*), George Frideric Handel

Piano Concerto no. 4 In G Minor (*Largo*), Sergei Rachmaninoff

Piano Sonata no. 20 in G, Op. 49 no. 2 (*Tempo di menuetto*), Ludwig van Beethoven

Piano Trio in A minor (*Andante con moto*), Peter Ilyich Tchaikovsky

Prelude in D, Sergei Rachmaninoff

Prelude no. 7 in A, Op. 28 (*Les Sylphides*), Frédéric Chopin

Waltz no. 15 in A-flat, Johannes Brahms

"Widmung" ("Dedication"), Franz Liszt

Sleepytime Selections

"Ave Verum Corpus," K. 618, Wolfgang Amadeus Mozart

"Canon," Johann Pachelbel

Horn Concerto no. 4 in E-flat—"Romanza" (*Andante*), Wolfgang Amadeus Mozart

Intermezzo no. 1 in E-flat, Johannes Brahms

"Lullaby," Johannes Brahms

"Maid with the Flaxen Hair," Claude Debussy

Minuet in G From the *Anna Magdalena Notebooks,* Johann Sebastian Bach

Orchestral Suite no. 3 in D, BWV 1068, "Air," Johann Sebastian Bach

Piano Concerto no. 15 in B-flat (*Andante*), Wolfgang Amadeus Mozart

Piano Concerto no. 21, K. 467 (*Andante*—Theme from *Elvira Madigan*), Wolfgang Amadeus Mozart

Piano Sonata no. 8 in C Minor, Op. 13 (*Adagio cantabile*— "Pathétique"), Ludwig van Beethoven

"Prelude to the Afternoon of a Faun," Claude Debussy

"Sanctus" (*from* Requiem Op. 48), Gabriel Faure

"Serenade for Winds," K. 375 (*Adagio*), Wolfgang Amadeus Mozart

"Sleepers, Awake:" From Cantata no. 140 ("Wachet auf, ruft uns die Stimme"), Johann Sebastian Bach

Symphony no. 9, *New World*, Antonin Dvorak

Symphony no. 38 "Prague" (*Andante*), Wolfgang Amadeus Mozart

"Wind Serenade" no. 12 in C minor (*Andante*), Wolfgang Amadeus Mozart

Main Index

Activity Level-Based Index

All-age activities

Products

Parents, especially first-time parents, can find themselves overwhelmed by the vast array of available learning tools for their children. Here's a small sampling of wonderful products for you to enjoy with your children.

Music

Baby Mozart™ Music Festival
Video/DVD
0-3 Years

"I work at a day care and my group of 2–3-year-olds are in love with the Baby Einstein videos, CDs, and books that I have for them. They're having so much fun they don't even realize that they're learning!"

Baby Vivaldi™
CD
All Ages

Art

baby einstein.
The ABCs of Art

COWS

C is for cows.

Do you think it is spring, summer, fall, or winter in this painting?

What does the artist use more: curvy lines or straight lines?

Language

Language Nursery
Video/DVD
Birth to 2 Years

Wordsworth's Book of Words
Picture Book
All Ages

Math and Science

Baby Newton™ Discovering Shapes
Video/DVD
1 Year & Up

Baby Newton™ Fun with Shapes
PC CD-ROM
1 Year & Up

Animals and Nature

Neighborhood Animals
Video/DVD
1 Year & Up

World Animals
Video/DVD
1 Year & Up

A child is **fascinated**
by the **world**.
You're fascinated by your **child**.
It may seem **simple**,
but that's only because **it is**.